Magic Tricks

Get started in a new craft with easy-to-follow

projects for beginners

PETER ELDIN

CHARTWELL
BOOKS, INC.

A QUINTET BOOK

Published by Chartwell Books
A Division of Book Sales, Inc.
114 Northfield Avenue
Edison, New Jersey 08837

This edition produced for sale
in the U.S.A., its territories
and dependencies only.

ISBN 0-7858-0570-2

This book was designed and produced by
Quintet Publishing Limited
6 Blundell Street
London N7 9BH

Creative Director: Richard Dewing
Designer: Bruce Low
Project Editor: Anna Briffa
Editor: Alison Leach
Photographer: Paul Forrester

Typeset in Great Britain by
Central Southern Typesetters, Eastbourne
Manufactured in Singapore by Eray Scan Pte Ltd
Printed in China by Leefung-Asco Printers Ltd

CONTENTS

INTRODUCTION

Generally, all books on magic explain the secret methods whereby the tricks are accomplished. This book is no exception. But let me tell you the greatest secret of magic – a secret that often takes magicians many years to discover, and which many never discover at all. That great secret is that the secret of a trick is the least important part of the trick!

In magic it matters little what you do. What matters most is how you do it. "It's not what you do but the way that you do

it" is an adage that is particularly appropriate to conjuring.

One of the tricks in this book is The Rising Cards, a trick that has baffled and entertained audiences all over the world. Many years ago a book was published describing some two hundred different methods of accomplishing this trick! Since that book was published, magicians have devised many more methods. The methods may vary but the essentials of the trick remain the same – selected cards rise from the pack of their own accord. So, no matter what method is used, the trick remains essentially the same. And that is why the so-called secrets of magic are not the most important part.

When reading the instructions for a trick, do not dismiss the method as being too simple. Some of the simplest of tricks are the most deceptive. Practice each trick and when you are sure that you can do it well, show it to a friend. You may be as amazed as your friend – amazed that such a simple method can fool someone.

Do not try to learn all the tricks at once. By all means read through the whole of this book to get a general idea of what magic is all about. Then pick just one or two tricks and learn them thoroughly. Only when you are confident that you can do these tricks well should you go on to learn another trick. It has been said that "Slow but sure wins the race," slow but sure is certainly the way to achieve success in performing magic.

None of the instructions given in this book is sacrosanct. If you are at all uncomfortable about a particular aspect of a trick, see if you can change it to suit your own style. An obvious example is where you are told to take something in a particular hand. If you are happier

using the other hand, then do so. No two magicians do the same trick in the same way – well, not if they have given any thought to their magic. One of the most interesting aspects of magic is that its performance is changing constantly.

At first you may go through the motions of a performance like a robot. But gradually, as you gain confidence and experience, the real you will come to the fore and your performances will be enhanced as a result.

It has been said that a good magician is really an actor playing the part of a magician. This means that you have got to believe in your magical abilities and to play the part of a magician. At first you may find this difficult to do because you are concentrating on the mechanics of the trick. That is why so many books on magic urge you to practice as much as possible. The emphasis is on the mechanics because the mechanics are unimportant. That may sound weird but the reason is that you must practice thoroughly, so the mechanics become automatic.

When you can do a trick without thinking, you can then concentrate on presenting your magic in a professional manner. It is somewhat similar to driving a car; at first the new driver is thinking, "Should I change gear or am I going at the wrong speed?" An experienced driver does not think, "Should I change gear?" He just does it. A better analogy might be with a tennis player who does not consciously think, "I must reach out to hit that ball and put some top spin on it to fool my opponent."

He just does it. It takes practice; and experience; it may even take a few knocks; but keep at it and you will get there in the end.

Many of the actual mechanics used by magicians are incredibly simple. It is even possible to buy tricks that are advertised as "self-working." The magician does not have to do anything – the trick does itself! Therein lies a danger. Tricks are often sold to tyro magicians with the assurance that there is "no skill required," or that the "trick is self-working." Don't believe it. There is no such thing as a self-working trick. If you want your magic to be successful, you have got to put work into it – even with "self-working" tricks. If you don't, you will just be someone performing tricks – a trained chimpanzee could do them just as well. But work at it, practice, make it

entertaining and a magical transformation takes place. No longer are you someone who just knows how to do a few tricks – you are a magician! Hard work always pays off in the end. The most important thing to remember is to imbue the trick with your own personality. You must be yourself, and you must perform in a way that is natural to you. This is not easy and it may take you some time before you can do it.

Please do not be a magic bore. You may like magic but the person you are boring may not. It is so easy to be a magic bore by showing trick after trick after trick. Keep to the old show-business saying, "Leave 'em wanting more." Just do one or two tricks at a time and people will come back. Do magic all night long and you could lose a lot of friends.

In this introduction you have been given quite a few dos and don'ts. Here comes the most important rule of them all: enjoy your magic. Don't take it too seriously. Have fun; that is what magic is all about.

MAGIC THROUGH THE AGES

No-one knows for certain how old the art of magic is. It is probably as old as mankind itself. The first actual record of a magical performance for entertainment purposes dates from the times of the Ancient Egyptians – but conjuring was a well-established art long before that.

In the early days there was very little difference between conjuring and witch-craft – indeed the terms get mixed up even today. The original performers called upon their knowledge of all the sciences and it is from the days of these witch-doctors/magicians/priests that most of the modern sciences originated. Somewhere along the way the magical entertainer left the mumbo jumbo of witchcraft and the intellectual pursuit of science behind and

began to ply his craft solely for the entertainment of others.

Even so these early performers were often accused of dark practices. The first book on conjuring in the English language was actually called *Discoverie of Witchcraft* but it explains many of the tricks that magicians still use to this day. One such trick is the Cups and Balls, in which balls appear and disappear beneath three cups. It is performed today using the same basic method described in *Discoverie of Witchcraft*. Its origins can be traced back to Ancient Rome, and it was probably known even earlier.

In the sixteenth century, when this book was published, the magicians were usually itinerant performers, doing their acts at

local fairs and markets. Then things began to change and performers were more often to be seen in theaters. Most magicians of this time wore long, flowing robes and their tables were draped to the ground. In the mid-nineteenth century a French performer called Robert-Houdin did away with all this suspicious drapery and performed in regular evening dress with very little paraphernalia on stage. Originally a watchmaker, he brought a new inventive-ness to magic. He built many automata which were used in his shows and he was one of the first people to do a two-person mind-reading act. His magic was so good the French government even employed him to prevent a revolution!

Robert-Houdin is regarded as "the father of modern conjuring" and it is from his name that young Ehrich Weiss took his stage name, a name that lives to this day – Houdini, the greatest escape artist ever. His first big success came when he escaped from handcuffs in Scotland Yard, the headquarters of the British police. From that time on he was constantly in the public eye, making incredible escapes from straitjackets, boxes, jails, handcuffs, chains, and anything else that people invented to try and confine him.

Contemporaries of Houdini included some of the greatest names in magic – Harry Kellar, who ran away from home to become America's best known illusionist; T. Nelson Downs, who produced showers of coins from the air; Harry Blackstone, who was a master showman and whose son is today one of America's best known magicians; and Chung Ling Soo, the renowned Chinese magician. Chung Ling Soo's greatest trick was not revealed until after his death. Everyone thought he was Chinese, he even used an interpreter, but after his death his great secret was revealed – he was really an American named William Robinson.

When Houdini first visited Britain, the top British magician was John Nevil Maskelyne. In addition to being a superb magician, Maskelyne was a genius at making mechanical figures. Possibly the most famous of these was called Psycho. This figure of an Oriental could play cards so well that it could beat any member of the audience offering the challenge. As the figure was seated on a plinth of clear glass, there seemed no logical explanation as to how the figure was operated. Maskelyne did not confine his mechanical genius to magic; he also invented a lock for public toilets, a typewriter and a machine for issuing bus tickets, among others!

Maskelyne teamed up with another British magician, David Devant and together they dominated the British magical scene for many years. People who saw Devant called him the greatest British magician of all time. That accolade has now passed down to Paul Daniels who has done more to popularize magic in Britain than any other person. For over 15 years he has had a regular magic series on television. His shows have also brought some of the best magicians from around the world to the attention of British audiences.

In recent years many incredible magical spectaculars have been produced, particularly in America with superb magicians such as Siegfried and Roy, David Copperfield, Harry Blackstone, Jr., and Lance Burton. These colorful extravaganzas use all the modern theatrical effects available and cost many millions of dollars to produce. In spite of all this hi-tec wizardry to excite the public, there is still room for the more intimate performance in small theaters, restaurants or informal gatherings. Magic can be performed for just one person or for many persons, but it is equally effective in any situation provided that the performer has taken the time to learn the art of entertaining people.

Coin in Ball of Yarn

The magician borrows a coin and makes it disappear. It is later recovered in the center of a ball of yarn.

You will need
◊ a ball of yarn
◊ a special "slide" (This is simply a flattened tin tube but it must be wide enough to take any coin you are likely to be offered.)
◊ a coin
◊ a glass tumbler

1 Wind the yarn around the bottom portion of the slide. Now place the ball of yarn in a left-side coat pocket or behind some piece of equipment on your table. It must be in a position that you can "load" the coin into the slide with your left hand and then pull the slide from the yarn without your actions being obvious.

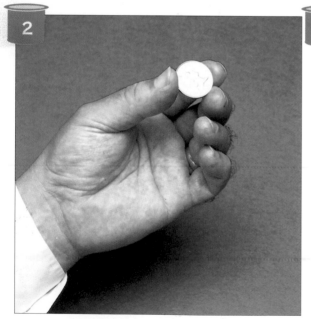

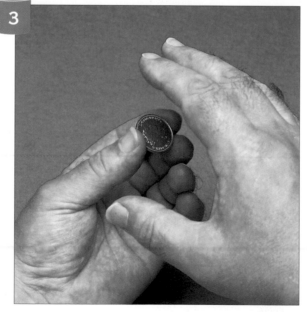

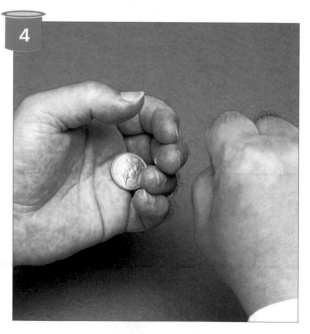

2 Borrow a coin from someone in your audience. Hold the coin between the tips of the thumb and forefinger of your left hand.

3 Bring your right hand over the coin as if to take it from the left. As soon as your right hand covers the coin, let the coin drop from your fingertips into the palm of your left hand.

4 As the coin drops, close your right hand as if taking the coin and move it away to the right. Look at your right hand as you do this and let your left hand fall away naturally.

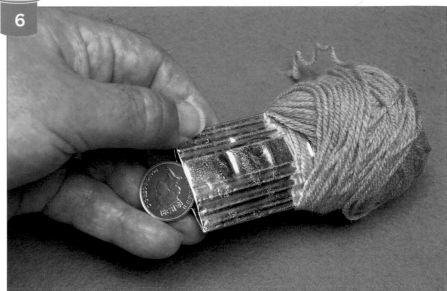

5 Make some comment about the fact that money does not last very long. Then, with a squeezing motion, open the fingers of your right hand. The coin has vanished! Try to forget that the coin is still hidden in your left hand. You must convince yourself that the coin has really vanished. If you do not convince yourself, you will not convince your audience.

TIP

• To prove that the coin revealed in the yarn is the very same coin that vanished, it is a good idea to have a small gummed sticker available. The spectator can stick this to the coin and sign it if so wished to prove that no substitution takes place. With an unusual coin, such as one of foreign currency, this will not be necessary.

6 While still gazing at your right hand in amazement, reach over with your left hand to recover the ball of yarn. Let the secreted coin enter the slide and then pull the slide out from the ball of yarn. With practice these movements should take only a moment.

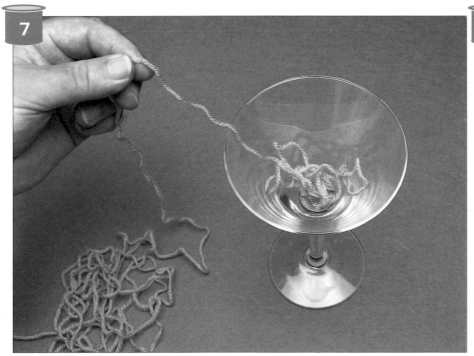

7 Show the ball of yarn to your audience and place it in the tumbler. Take hold of the end of the yarn and pull it from the tumbler. When the yarn is completely unraveled, the coin will tinkle into the tumbler.

8 Hand the tumbler to the person from whom you borrowed the coin and ask if it is the very same coin.

CARD CONTROL

A playing card is chosen by a spectator who then returns it to the pack. Even though the pack is thoroughly shuffled, the magician reveals the identity of the selected card in a surprising manner.

You will need
◊ a pack of cards

1 Shuffle the cards and then fan them out, face down, between your hands and ask someone to take any card.

2 Gather the remaining cards together and hold the pack in the left hand. As the spectator is looking at the card, lift off about two-thirds of the pack with your right hand. Ask the spectator to return the chosen card to the lower portion of the pack.

3 Replace the top portion of the cards but first place the tip of your left little finger on the chosen card. Although the pack is now reassembled, your little finger holds a "break" at the rear end of the pack.

4 Lift off about one-third of the cards immediately with your right hand and place them on the table.

5 Next lift off all the cards above your little finger and place them on top of the cards on the table.

6 Finally, place the bottom portion of the pack on top of the cards on the table. It appears that the chosen card is now completely lost in the pack but, unbeknown to the audience, it is actually the top card.

7 Pick up the pack and give it an overhand shuffle. This is a perfectly fair shuffle except for the fact that the first card is taken singly from the pack into the left hand.

8 The remaining cards are then shuffled on top of the first card. The shuffle looks perfectly normal but the chosen card is now on the bottom of the pack.

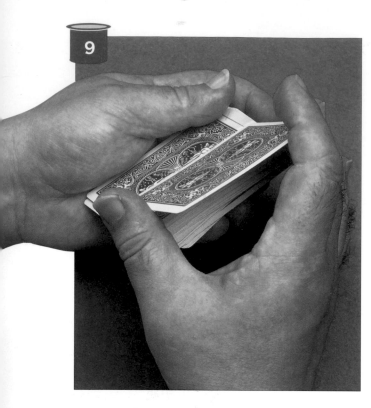

9 Shuffle the cards again until you reach the bottom portion of the pack. As you finish the shuffle, make sure that the final part of the shuffle consists of a single card (the bottom chosen card) only. Unbeknown to the spectators, the chosen card is now back on top of the pack.

10 As you know the location of the chosen card, there are several ways in which you can reveal its identity.

a) Fan the faces of the cards toward yourself for a brief second as if concentrating. You simply look at the top card of the pack and you can now appear to read the spectator's mind as you name the chosen card.

b) Hold the pack behind your back and say that you will try to locate the chosen card through the power of your magic fingers. Pretend to be searching through the cards and then bring forward the top card – it is the spectator's selection!

c) Ask another spectator to choose a card. But this time you do not allow a free choice – you force the top card . When both spectators are asked to name their chosen cards, they both name the same card – an amazing coincidence.

TIP

• As with all tricks, you must practice this until you can do all the moves convincingly and naturally. Do not give the appearance of doing something difficult. The shuffling process must be exactly the same as you would use if you were shuffling the cards normally.

CARD THROUGH HANDKERCHIEF

A card is selected and returned to the center of the pack. The cards are then shuffled before being wrapped in a handkerchief. When the handkerchief is shaken, one card penetrates through the fabric – it is the selected card.

You will need
◊ a pack of cards
◊ a handkerchief

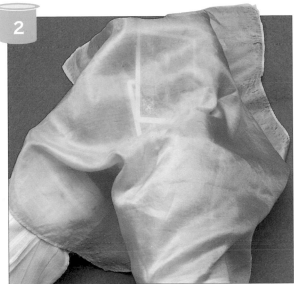

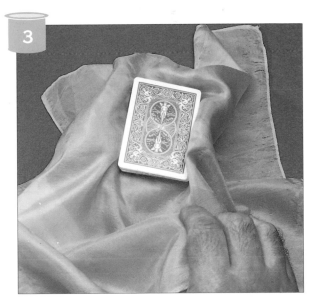

1 Have a card selected and returned to the pack. Secretly bring the chosen card to the top of the pack as described in Card Control on pages 10-12.

2 Hold the pack in your left hand and drape the handkerchief over it. Immediately the pack is covered, your right hand reaches beneath the handkerchief, retrieves the pack, and places it on top of the fabric. Unbeknown to the audience, the top card has been left behind, resting on the palm of your left hand.

3 Grasp the edge of the handkerchief nearest your body and lift it up and forward to cover the pack.

4 Your right hand now takes the pack between finger and thumb, holding it through the fabric.

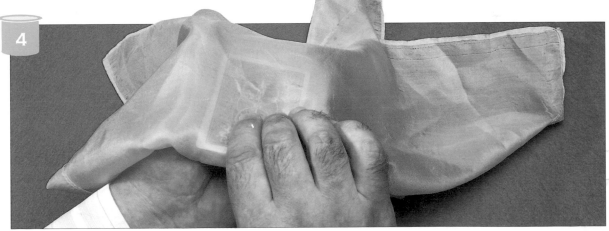

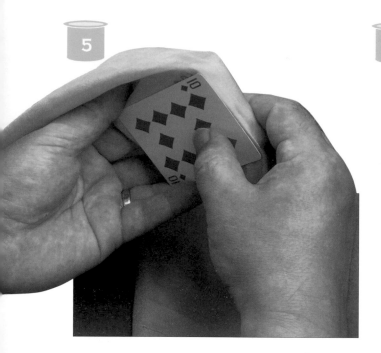

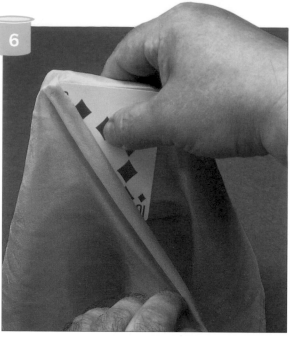

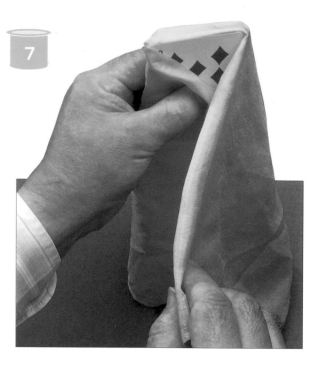

5 The selected card remains hidden beneath the handkerchief, held in position by your right thumb.

6 Your left hand now takes the left edge of the handkerchief and wraps the fabric backward and around the rear of the pack.

7 Transfer the pack (and hidden card) to your left hand, still holding it through the fabric. This leaves your right hand free to drape the right side of the fabric back and around the pack.

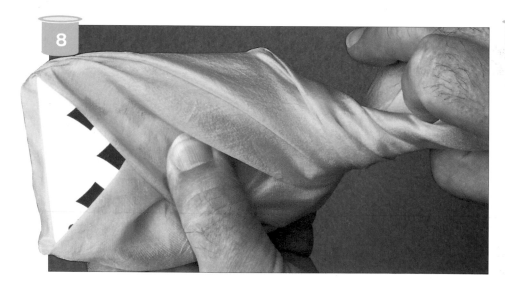

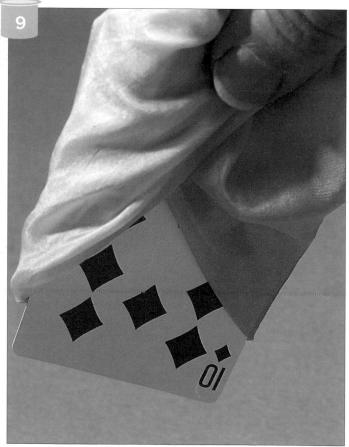

8 Take all the fabric hanging beneath the pack and twist it around several times. The pack is now completely enclosed by the fabric and the selected card is held in a pocket formed by the way the pack is wrapped. Move your right hand upward and your left down, then remove your left hand.

9 Ask the spectator to name the selected card and then begin shaking your right hand. The selected card will gradually come into view and appears to be penetrating the fabric.

RING OFF ROPE

A finger ring is threaded onto a length of rope. Even though both ends of the rope are held by spectators, the magician manages to take the ring off the rope.

You will need
◊ a short length (about 1 yard) of rope or string

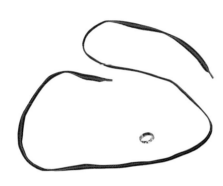

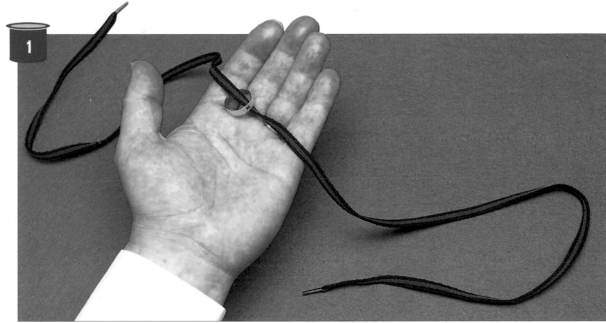

1 Ask if you can borrow a finger ring from someone in the audience. Thread the rope through the ring and display the ring on the palm of your left hand.

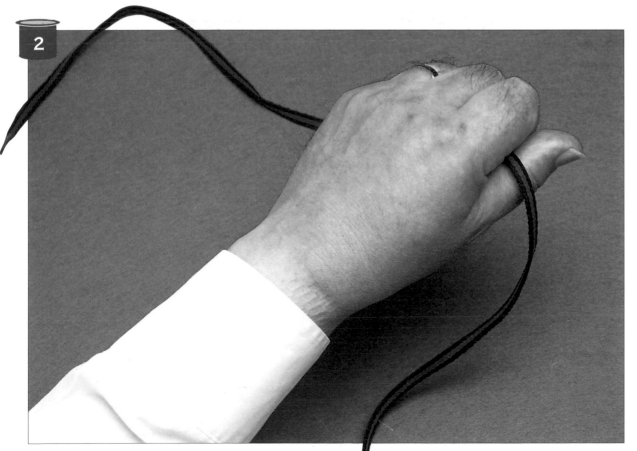

2 Close your left hand and turn it over so your fingers face the floor.

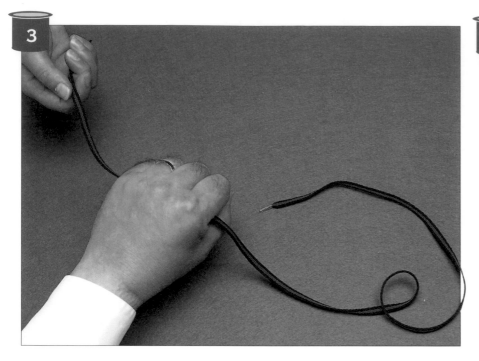

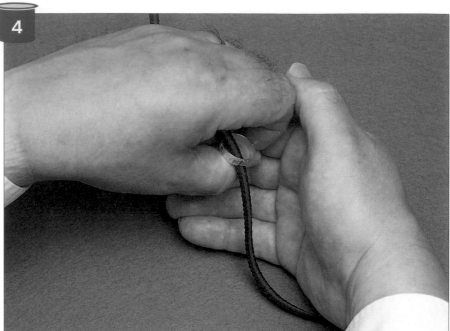

3 As your left hand is turned over, your right hand comes in front of it and grasps the rope to the left. Your right hand continues to the left and gives the left end of the rope to a spectator to hold.

4 Your right hand is now moved back to the right to give the right end of the rope to another spectator. It is here that the secret move that accomplishes the trick takes place. As your right hand passes beneath your left to get hold of the rope near to your left thumb, your left hand opens slightly to let the ring fall into your passing right hand.

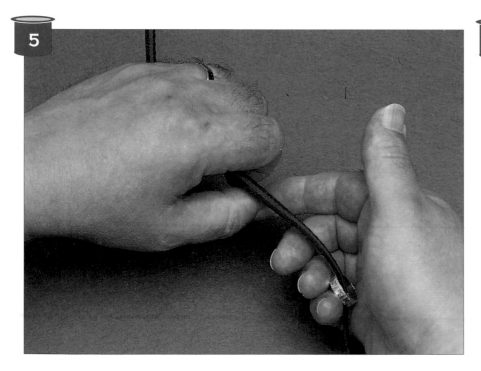

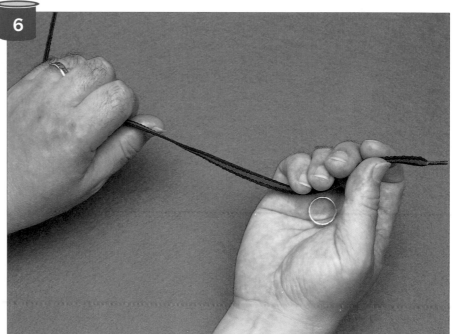

5 Your right hand continues toward the right end of the rope with the ring concealed.

6 Just before your right hand reaches the end of the rope, look to the spectator on the left and ask for the rope to be held slightly higher. To emphasize this, you raise your left hand. At this precise moment your right hand moves farther to the right and takes the ring off the rope.

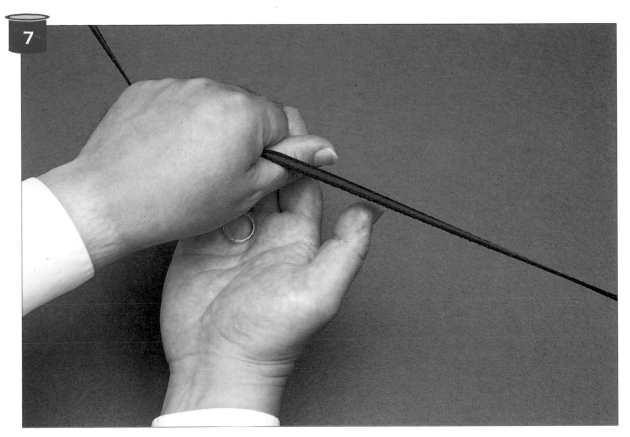

7 Your right hand, keeping the ring hidden, then picks up the right end of the rope and gives it to someone on your right. Now both ends of the rope are being held tight by spectators. The ring is still in your right hand.

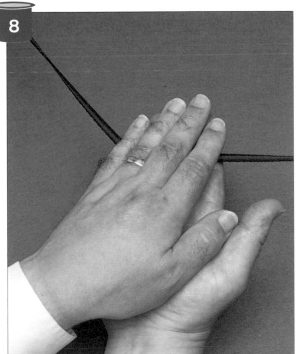

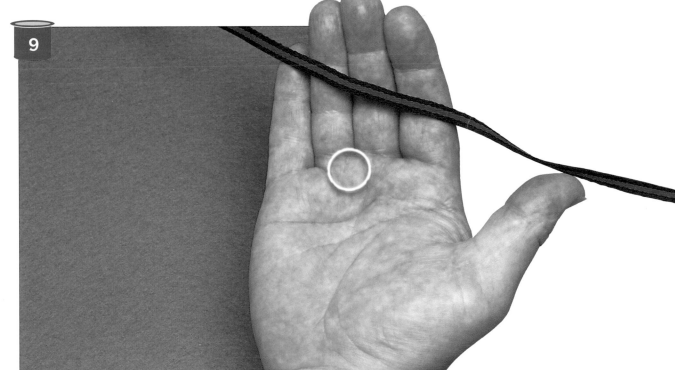

8 Look at your left hand, which is apparently still holding the ring, and start a squeezing motion as if you are trying to maneuver the ring through the solid rope. Bring your right hand under your left and place both hands palm to palm.

9 Roll your palms together for a moment and then lift your left hand to reveal the ring on your right. It seems that the ring has penetrated the rope.

RING ON PENCIL

A finger ring, borrowed from a spectator, vanishes and reappears on the center of a pencil.

You will need

◊ a special "vanishing" handkerchief
◊ a paper bag
◊ a long pencil

1 To make the special handkerchief required for this trick, you will need, in addition to the handkerchief itself, a piece of matching fabric, a metal ring, and needle and thread.

Cut a small triangle from the extra fabric and sew it onto one corner of the handkerchief. Before sewing up the third side, place the ring in the pocket you have formed. Sew up the third side to enclose the ring and your preparation is complete.

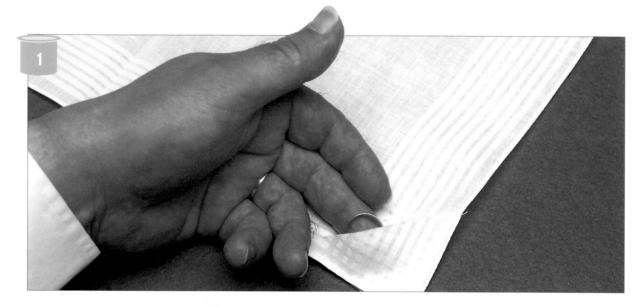

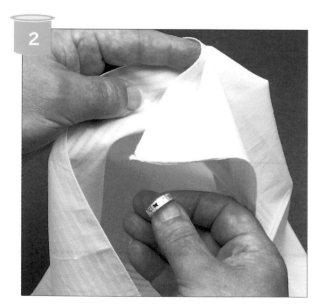

2 In performance you first borrow a finger ring from a member of the audience. Hold the ring between the thumb and first finger of your left hand and then drape the handkerchief over it.

3 You now hand the handkerchief to a second person with the request that he or she guard it safely. In actual fact you now have the ring in your possession. This is how you get it. As you approach the second spectator, your right hand takes the corner of the handkerchief containing the secret ring and puts it up into your left fingers. At the same time the borrowed ring is allowed to drop from your left hand into the right.

4 Hand the handkerchief to the second spectator, asking him or her to keep hold of the ring. In fact it is the secret ring that the spectator is holding. This is the reason why you do not use the owner of the ring for this part of the trick as he or she might determine by touch that the ring in the handkerchief is not his or her own ring.

TIP
• A similar handkerchief with a coin in the pocket can be used to make a coin disappear.

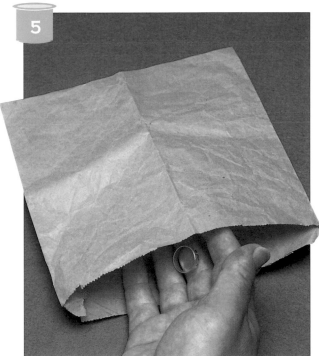

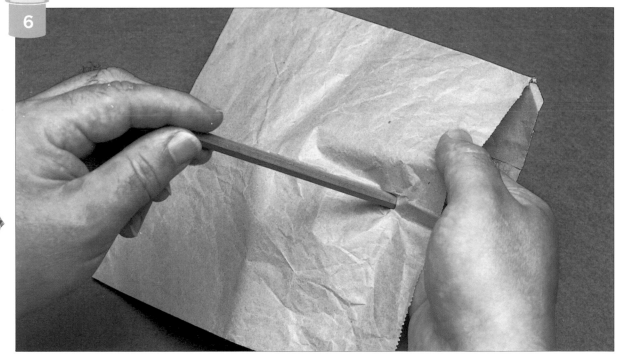

5 With your right hand concealing the ring, reach over to the paper bag that is lying on your table. Do this naturally and casually and do not look at your right hand as you do this. If you look at your hand, you will draw attention to it and this could arouse suspicions in the minds of the audience. Try to forget the fact that you have a ring in your hand. If you start worrying about it, you could transmit your unease and that would spoil the effect.

6 Holding the bag in your right hand, reach in with your left to take out the pencil. In a subtle way this "proves" that the bag is otherwise empty. Do not mention the fact that the bag is empty, because by doing so you would only draw attention to it.

Now push the pencil through one side of the bag and out the other. In so doing, you push the pencil through the hidden ring. Remove your right hand from the bag and screw up the top of the bag.

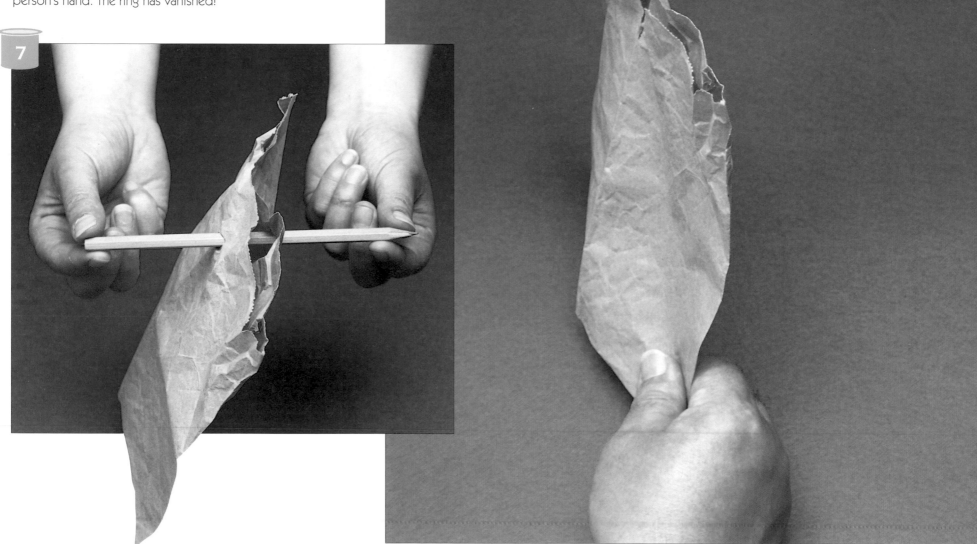

7 Hand the pencil to the spectator from whom you borrowed the ring with the request that he or she holds each end of it. Go back to the second spectator who is still holding the handkerchief. Take one corner of the handkerchief and pull it from the person's hand. The ring has vanished!

8 Go back to the first person and pull the bag downward to reveal the ring on the center of the pencil. Ask the owner to confirm that it is indeed his or her ring and thank both of your assistants for their help.

THE COIN FOLD

A coin is wrapped in a piece of paper from where it disappears.

You will need
◊ a coin
◊ a square sheet of paper

1 This is a superb trick to perform on the spur of the moment for the coin can be borrowed and the paper can be simply a square torn from a newspaper (or whatever else is available). Place the coin on the center of the square of paper.

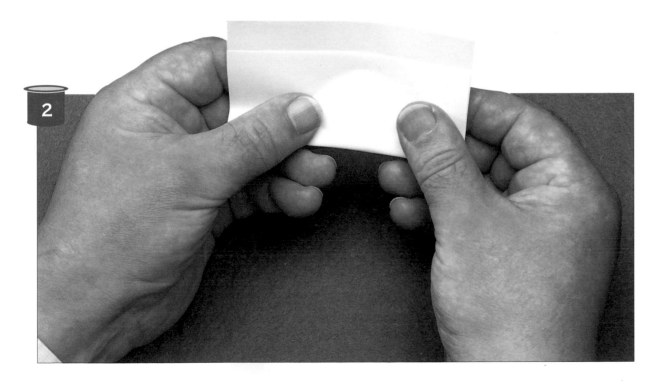

2 Fold the bottom edge of the paper up and over the coin. Do not bring the bottom edge right up to meet the top edge but about ¾ inch below it.

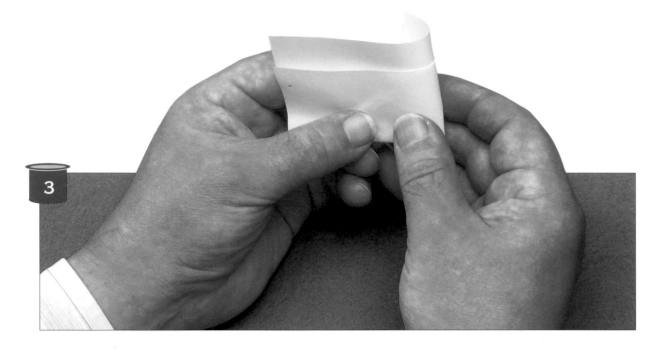

3 Fold the right edge of the paper back behind the coin.

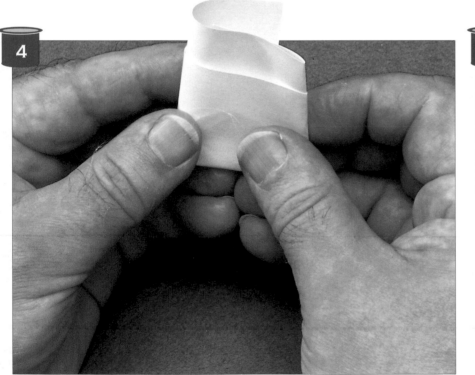

4 Fold the left edge back and behind the coin.

5 For the final fold, bend the top flap of paper back behind the coin. It appears that the coin is secure in the paper but in fact the top edge is open.

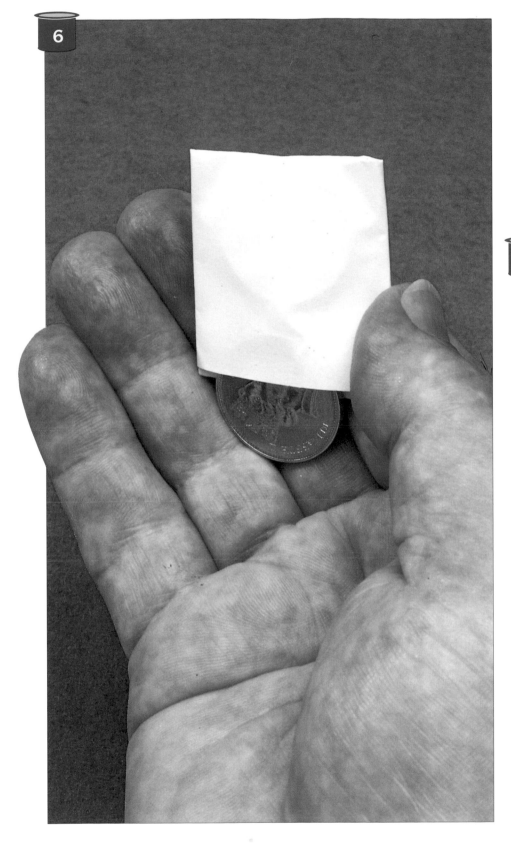

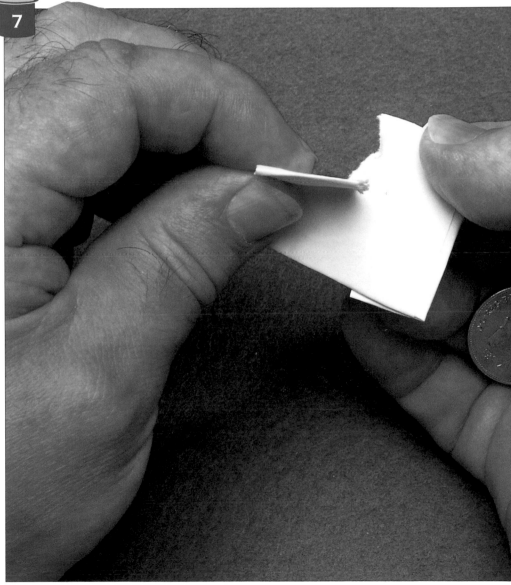

6 Turn the paper around so that the open edge is toward the bottom. The coin can now slip from its paper prison into your right hand.

7 Tear up the paper and throw the pieces on the table. The coin has apparently vanished but, in reality, remains concealed in your right hand.

A CAPITAL PREDICTION

The performer shows a bag containing numerous slips of paper on which are written the names of capital cities. Some of the slips are removed from the bag and the names called out to give some indication of the range available. Finally, one slip is withdrawn from the bag and the chosen capital named. A large envelope, which has been on view throughout, is then opened to reveal a card bearing the name of the chosen city.

You will need
◊ a change bag (a utility prop that can be used for hundreds of tricks)
◊ about 100 slips of paper measuring approximately 3 x 1¼ inches
◊ ball-point pen or typewriter
◊ a piece of card
◊ a large envelope

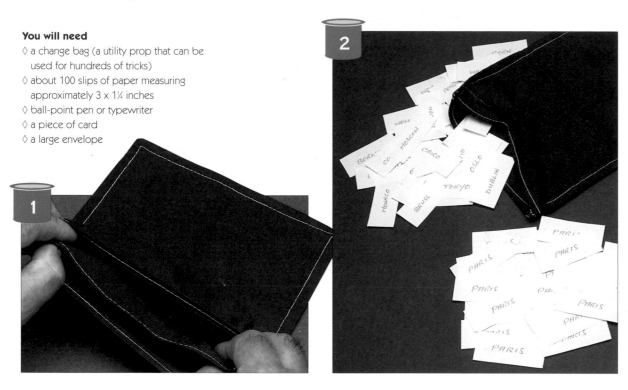

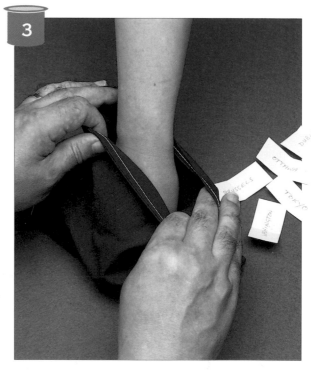

1 A change bag is simply a cloth bag in which there is a central divider. As the audience is not aware of this, it is possible to put something into the bag (putting it into one of the compartments) and then show the bag empty (by showing the other compartment). The easiest way to make such a bag is to take a strip of fabric measuring approximately 20 x 8 inches. Fold the fabric into three and then sew down the sides and bottom to make the bag. An even simpler change bag can be made by gluing two paper bags together.

2 On 50 slips of paper write the name of one capital city. Let's use Paris as an example. Fold these slips of paper in half and drop all into one side of your bag. Write the names of different capital cities on each of the remaining 50 slips. Fold these in half and place them in the other compartment of the bag. Write the name Paris on the card, place this in the large envelope, and you are ready to perform.

3 Show the envelope to the audience and place it in a position where it can be observed by them. Pick up the change bag, reach into the compartment with the different cities and pull out a handful of slips. Let them fall from your fingers and then let them fall back into the bag as you say, "I have here over a hundred [magic is all about lying] slips of paper bearing the names of capital cities and I would like one of them to be chosen." Invite someone up to assist you and ask that person to draw out a few slips from the bag, unfold them and call out the names of the cities written on them.

24

TIP

• There are literally hundreds of tricks that can be done with a change bag: three colored handkerchiefs, dropped into the bag, become knotted together; a sheet of paper torn into pieces and dropped into the bag is magically restored; a long piece of rope is dropped into the bag and when it is removed, there are lots of knots along its length; and many, many more.

4 You now explain that this time you want just one slip to be taken. While you are talking, alter the positions of your fingers on the bag so that next time you open it, the spectator reaches into the other compartment (the one in which all the slips bear the same name).

5 One slip is chosen and the name read out (it is, of course, Paris). Emphasize that the spectator had a perfectly free choice (another lie) and draw attention to the envelope that has been on view throughout.

6 When the envelope is opened, it is seen that you accurately predicted which capital city would be chosen.

DRINK FROM NOWHERE

A handkerchief is shown on both sides and then draped over the magician's hand.
Suddenly, a form appears beneath the fabric. When the handkerchief is removed, there,
standing on the magician's hand, is a wineglass – full of wine!

You will need
◊ some wine, fruit juice, or other liquid
◊ a wineglass
◊ a sheet of strong kitchen wrap (large enough
  to cover the mouth of the glass)
◊ an elastic band
◊ a handkerchief

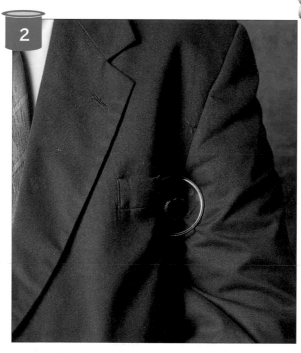

1 Pour the liquid into the glass and cover the glass with the kitchen wrap. Use the elastic band to hold the wrap in place. The elastic band must be tight enough to hold the wrap securely but with sufficient elasticity to enable you to remove it easily without fumbling. You will have to experiment to find the right band for the glass you are using.

2 Now place the glass in your left armpit, with the bottom of the glass facing the audience. Adjust the fabric of your clothing to cover as much of the base as possible. Because of this positioning of the glass, this trick has to be the opening one in your performance.

3 Walk onto the stage and display the handkechief between your hands.

4 Now bring your left hand forward and to the right as your right hand moves to the left. This movement lets you show the other side of the handkerchief. It also brings your right hand in the correct position to "steal" the glass from its hiding place.

5 Grip the stem of the glass between the second and third fingers of your right hand and then move your hands back to their opening position, with the handkerchief spread out between them. The glass is now hidden behind the top right corner of the handkerchief.

6 Let go of the right corner as your right hand moves to the center of the material. At the same time use your left hand to smooth the fabric out over your right palm. Because the glass is still hanging from your fingers, there is no indication that anything has happened.

7 Your left fingers now grip the center of the handkerchief and lift it upward. At the same time your right hand swivels the glass into an upright position.

8 Your left hand is now lowered and the fact that something has appeared beneath the handkerchief is immediately apparent to the audience.

9 Your left fingers, working through the fabric, pull the elastic band and cover off the glass, and then pull the handkerchief away. The glass is revealed and while attention is on this, put the handkerchief, with the cover and band hidden inside, quickly to one side.

THE RISING CARDS

This is one of the classics of magic – three chosen cards rise from the pack of their own accord.

You will need
◊ a pack of cards
◊ razor blade or sharp knife
◊ about 1 yard of fine black thread
◊ a glass tumbler that will hold a pack of cards
◊ a small tray

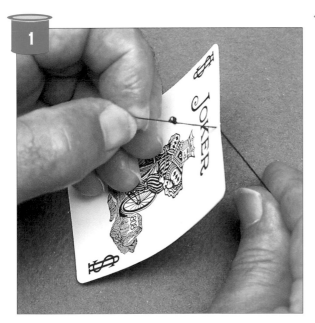

1 Take one card and cut a slit in one end of it using a razor blade or sharp knife. Push one end of the cotton through the slits and tie several knots in the end.

2 Place one card face down on your table and the prepared card face down on top of it. The slit in the prepared card should be facing toward the back of the table. The thread hangs down from the card onto the floor. The tumbler and the rest of the pack are in front of the face-down cards.

3 When you wish to do the trick, pick up the pack and give the cards a shuffle. Ask three spectators each to take a card. They keep their cards while you return to your table. Place the pack down on top of the two cards already there.

4

4 Pick up the glass and show it to the audience. Put the glass back on the table and pick up the pack. Place the pack in the glass in such a way that the thread runs from the front of the pack, across the top of the cards, and then down to the floor.

5

6

5 Collect the chosen cards on the tray and then place them, one by one, into the pack. This action pushes the thread down to the bottom of the pack.

6 Place your foot on the thread on the floor (it may help to stick a small pellet of paper to the end of the thread to enable you to spot it more easily). Lift up the glass and ask for the names of the three cards. As the glass is lifted, the thread is tautened and the cards will rise from the pack one by one.

ON THE TIP OF MY TONGUE

A comedy card trick. The magician tries some mind-reading and fails . . . but not for long.

You will need
◊ a pack of cards
◊ a piece of paper upon which is written "six of clubs"
◊ a handkerchief

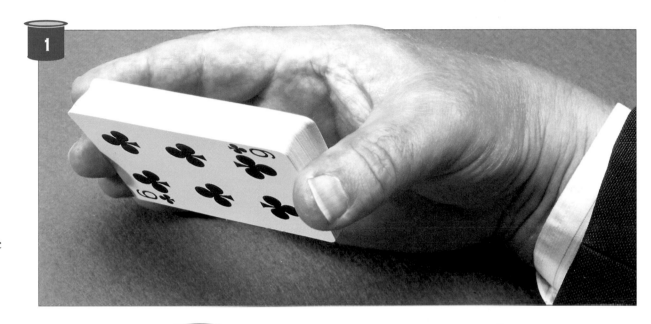

1 Put the six of clubs (or whichever card you decide to use) on the bottom of the pack. Put the pack and the handkerchief on the table. Hide the piece of paper in some place where you can retrieve it easily without anyone noticing.

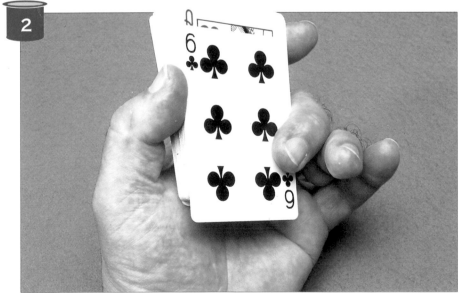

2 Pick up the pack with your right hand and cover it with the handkerchief. As you are arranging the fabric of the handkerchief, use your right fingers to pull the bottom card slightly to one side. (For the sake of clarity the handkerchief has been removed in the photographs.)

3 You then say that you want someone to lift off a portion of cards through the fabric and then to reach beneath the handkerchief and take the next card from the pack. You demonstrate this by lifting off some cards but in fact you actually lift all the cards except the bottom one. (This is quite easy to do because the bottom card is out of alignment.)

31

4 This lets you turn the bottom card, which is still on your left hand, face up.

5 Put the pack together again and let the spectator lift off some cards. As soon as this is done, you secretly turn the bottom half over.

6 When the spectator reaches beneath the hand-kerchief to take the "next" card, it is the reversed card that is taken.

7 As soon as the card has been taken, turn the bottom half of the pack back the right way and let the spectator replace the top half. It appears that the spectator has had a free choice of card but the card has actually been "forced."

8 Place the pack and handkerchief back down on the table and ask the spectator to show the chosen card to the rest of the audience. While all attention is on this action, retrieve the piece of paper and put it in your mouth. Rest it on your tongue.

9 Announce that you will now read the spectator's mind and will reveal the name of the chosen card. You then make a few inaccurate guesses as to the identity of the card. Annoyed at this lack of success, you say, "I don't know what's wrong with me today. A second ago I had the name of your card on the tip of my tongue." As you say this, put out your tongue to reveal the paper. Take the paper from your mouth and show the writing — you really did have the spectator's card on the tip of your tongue!

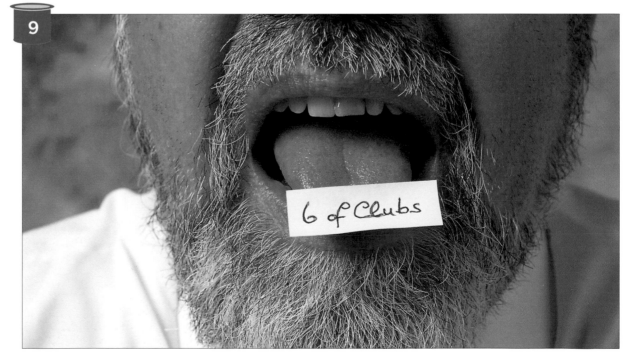

SUN AND MOON

Two squares of paper, one red and one yellow, have their centers removed. The magician restores them but the red center is now in the yellow square and the yellow center is in the red square. The magician's powers are once again conjured up and this time the two squares of paper are restored correctly.

You will need
◊ a card template, ⅛ of a circle
◊ four squares of red paper
◊ four squares of yellow paper
◊ scissors
◊ glue
◊ paper clip
◊ a change bag (as described on page 24)

1 Fold one square of each color in half lengthways then widthways to form a smaller square. Fold this diagonally to give a triangle. Use the template to cut a circle from each triangle. For descriptive purposes we will call the cutout circles R1 (for red) and Y1 (for yellow). Keep the circles and discard the rest of each square.

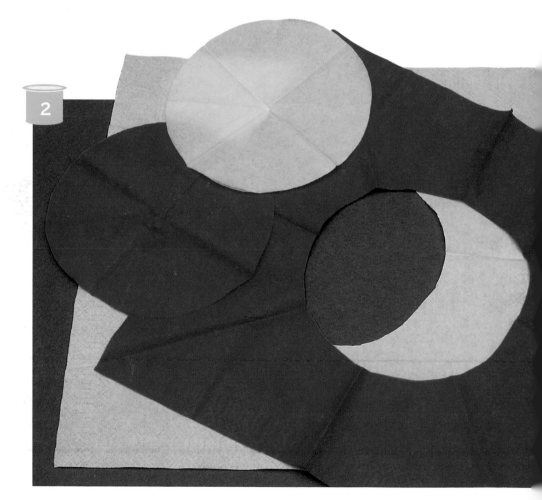

2 Cut two slightly smaller circles from the centers of two other squares of paper (again, one red and one yellow). Discard the circles you have cut out and then glue R1 onto the hole in the yellow square and Y1 onto the hole in the red square. You now have a yellow square with a red circle in its center and a red square with a yellow circle in its center.

3 When the glue has dried, fold the two prepared squares into four and put a paper clip over them. Now put them in the front compartment of a change bag. Alongside them, place two ordinary squares (one red and one yellow) similarly folded. The two remaining squares are also folded into four and placed on your table. Before placing the squares on the table, draw part of a circle in pencil on their centers (using the same card template you used earlier). You are now ready to perform. Pick up the squares from the table and display them. Now use the scissors to cut a circle from the center of each paper (use your penciled guidelines to get the cutting more or less the right size).

4 Show the two squares with the holes in them and then show the two paper circles. Fold them all up and put them into the back pocket of the change bag. Say a few magic words and then place your hand in the front compartment of the bag. Find the papers with the paper clip, pull off the clip, and bring them into view.

5 You claim to have restored the papers but when they are unfolded, it seems you have gone terribly wrong – the yellow paper has a red circle in its center and the red a yellow circle.

6 Fold up the faulty papers (or tear them up first if you wish) and put them into the rear compartment of the change bag.

7 This time you use some stronger magic words before reaching into the front compartment of the bag to remove the papers therein. Open out the papers and they are seen to be fully restored – another miracle accomplished!

SOLID THROUGH SOLID

Two colored handkerchiefs are wrapped around one another until it is absolutely impossible for them to be parted. The magician blows on them and the handkerchiefs appear to melt through one another.

You will need
◊ two colored handkerchiefs

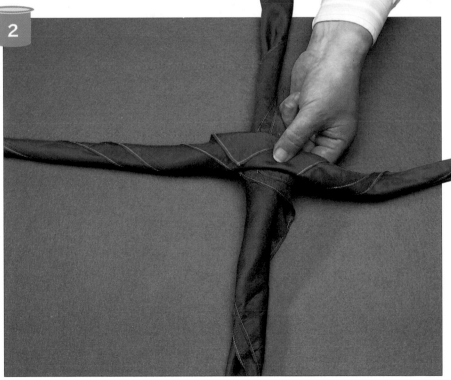

1 For the purposes of description we will assume that one handkerchief is purple and the other is red, although the actual colors are immaterial. Take the diagonally opposite corners of each handkerchief and roll the fabric into a tube shape. Place the purple handkerchief on the table and then lay the red one across it at 90 degrees.

2 Pick up the handkerchiefs where they cross between the thumb and fingers of your hand.

3 Your right hand now approaches from the right and goes beneath the purple handkerchief to take hold the left end of the red handkerchief.

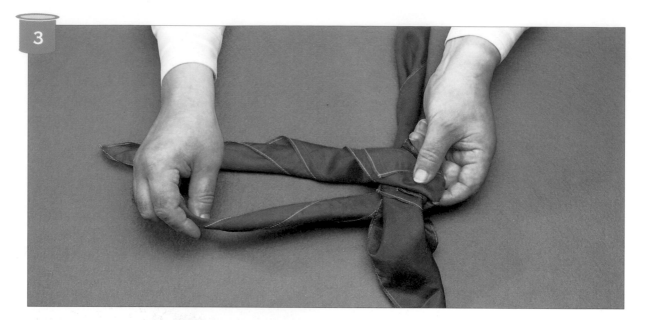

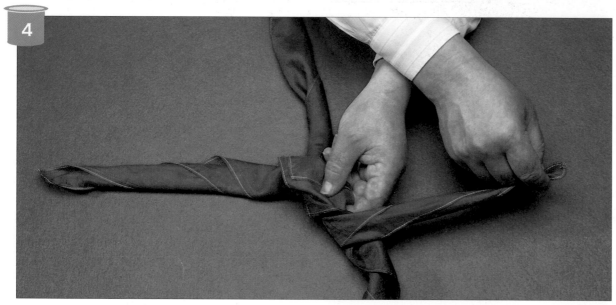

4 This end is then taken to the right, below the purple handkerchief and then back to the left over the top of the purple.

5 Now take the nearest end of the purple handkerchief below and then back over the red.

6

7

6 Hold the two ends of the red handkerchief together and the two purple ends together. It looks as if the handkerchiefs are inextricably locked together.

7 Blow gently on the handkerchiefs (to make the magic work) and then pull your hands apart. Amazingly, the two handkerchiefs separate!

CUT AND RESTORED ROPE

A length of rope is cut into two pieces and then restored to one by the magician.

You will need
◊ a small piece of rope
◊ transparent adhesive tape
◊ a good length of rope
◊ a handkerchief
◊ scissors

1 Take the smaller piece of rope and form it into a small loop using the tape to hold the join. Place the loop over the long piece of rope and lay both on your table, using the handkerchief or something else to conceal the ring from the spectators' view. In performance you pick up the rope with your right hand. Your hand actually goes around the loop

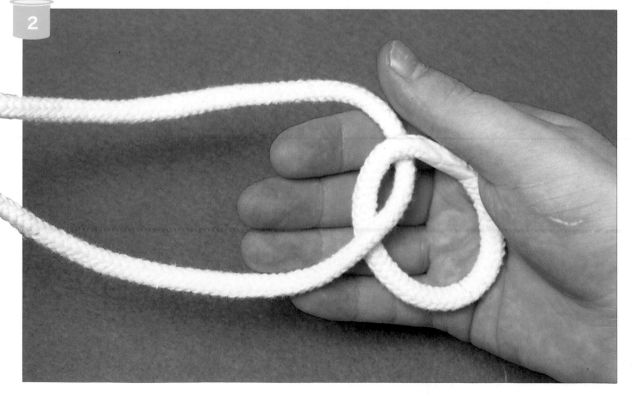

2 Take the bottom end of the rope in your left hand and hold the rope between your hands. (This gives the audience the impression that you are holding a single length of rope – they have no knowledge of the loop of rope concealed by the fingers of your right hand.)

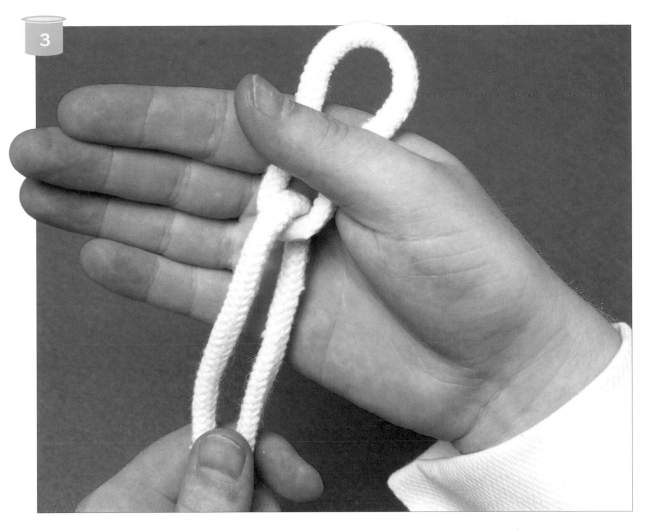

3 Lift your left hand upward toward the end of the rope held in your right hand. Your left hand now grasps the end above your right hand and your right hand moves down to the center of the rope (taking the hidden loop with it). Let go of the rope ends held in your left hand as your right hand moves upward (apparently to show the center of the rope but by this time part of the loop has been allowed to come into view).

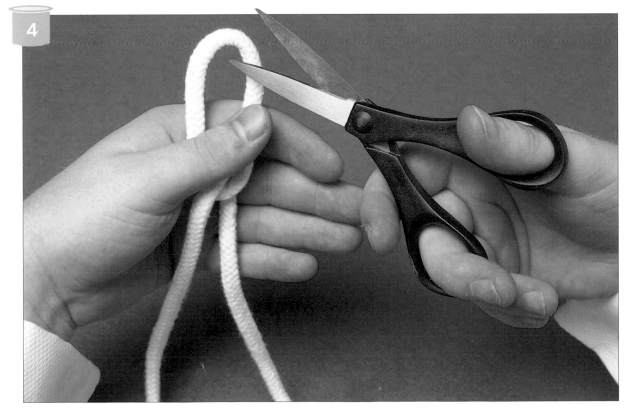

4 Transfer what appears to be the center of the rope from your right hand into your left (being careful not to reveal the loop). Do not make anything special of this movement. It should appear that you have simply transferred the center of the rope from one hand to the other so that you can pick up the scissors with your right hand. Take the scissors in your right hand and apparently cut through the center of the rope (in fact you are just cutting through the extra loop of rope).

5

5 It now appears that you have two pieces of rope in your hand because the spectators can see two ends above your left hand and two ends at the lower position.

6

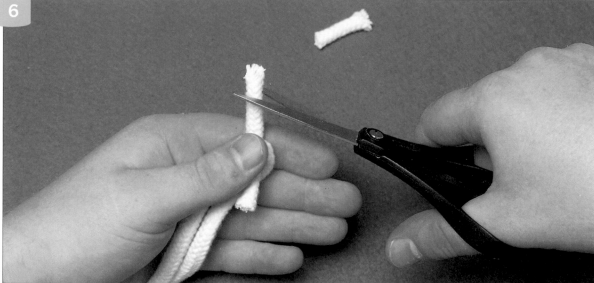

6 Use the scissors to "trim" the top ends (but actually you trim off so much that you cut away all of the secret loop).

7

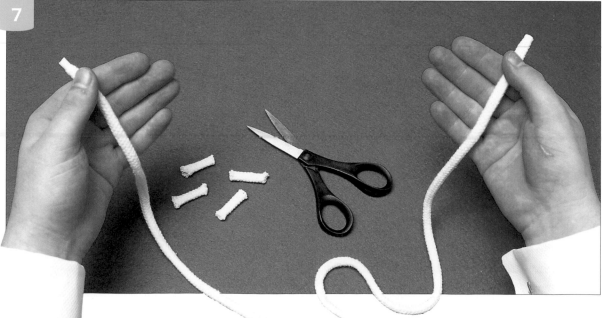

7 Put the scissors down. Wave your right hand over the "cut" center of the rope. Bring both hands out to the ends of the rope and show the completely restored rope as you take your bow.

BANK NIGHT

Four envelopes numbered 1 to 4 are shown. The magician explains that one of them contains some money and that three lucky people will be given the chance to win it. Three envelopes are chosen by spectators, leaving the magician with just one. When the spectators open their envelopes they are seen to be unlucky. The magician opens the remaining, unchosen envelope, and wins the cash!

You will need
◊ four numbered envelopes
◊ a large denomination bill
◊ four pieces of paper the same size as the bill

1 Before your performance place a piece of paper in each envelope. Seal the envelopes and number them 1 to 4. The numbering can be done with a pen, be printed, or use numbered gummed stickers available from most stationers.

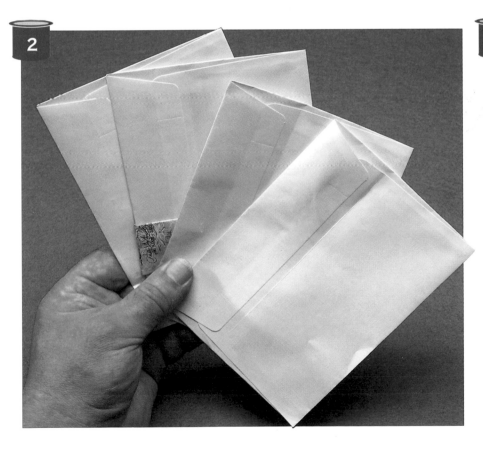

2 Place the envelopes in a fan shape (in numerical order) on your table, envelope number 1 being to the left of the fan. Fold the bill into four and slip it onto the left edge of envelope number 2. Now turn all the envelopes over to conceal the bill beneath them.

3 In performance pick up the envelopes between your left thumb and forefinger and turn them so that the numbers are facing the audience. The concealed bill will be visible to you but hidden from the audience's view.

4 You now let each of three spectators select an envelope by calling out its number. Whichever number is chosen, you pull it from the fan and hand it to the spectator. It is important that you keep the bill concealed behind the fingers of your left hand as you do this.

5 When you are left with just one envelope, hold it with the bill still hidden behind it.

6 Ask the spectators if they wish to change their envelopes. They can exchange with one another or they can exchange with you. If they exchange with one another, you have nothing to worry about. If someone wants to exchange with you, take their envelope and place it in front of the envelope you hold. Then remove your envelope and hand it to the spectator. In this way the bill remains hidden at all times.

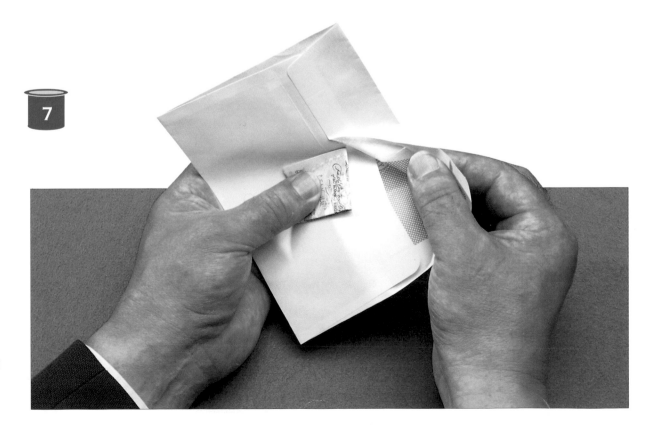

7 Ask the spectators to open their envelopes to see if they have won – unfortunately, they have not! Keeping then bill hidden, begin to open your envelope.

8 Place your right fingers into your envelope. Your thumb goes behind the envelope and onto the bill. Now move your hand to the right, pulling the note to the right with your thumb.

TIP

• Instead of leaving the envelopes empty, each could contain a little note of consolation which each spectator is asked to read out. Suitable phrases include "Money isn't everything," "You can't win them all," "Better luck next time," and so on. If you can come up with some amusing phrases, so much the better as this will add a little light comedy to the proceedings.

9 As your fingers clear the envelope, the bill, held between fingers and thumb, becomes visible to the audience. The illusion of it coming from the envelope is absolutely perfect – and you appear to have won the money!

SEE-THROUGH PRODUCTION

A box is shown completely empty, then the magician proceeds to produce a variety of handkerchiefs and colored streamers from it.

You will need

◊ a square box with an open front
◊ a tube glued inside the box
◊ a square tube (small enough to fit into the box but large enough to go over the fixed tube)
◊ silk scarves, ribbons, paper streamers, etc.

2 In performance you just lift out the square tube and show it to be empty. At this point, although you must not draw attention to the fact, the audience can see through the cutout in the front of the box. Because the interior is black and the inner tube is also black, it seems that the box is empty.

1 Put the ribbons, streamers, or whatever else is to be produced into the inner tube. Place the square tube into the box.

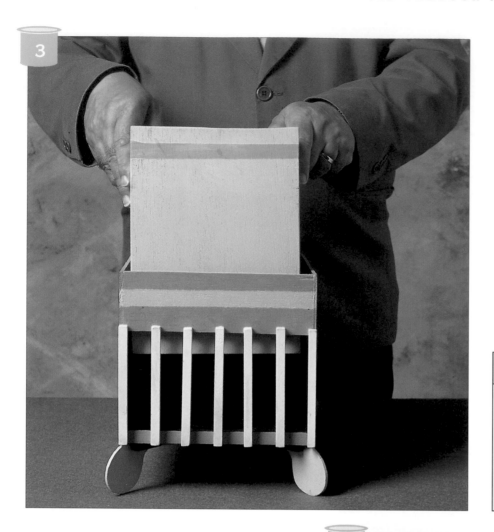

3 Place the square tube back in position.

4 Wave your hands over the boxes in a mystical manner and then reach in to produce the scarves, handkerchiefs, colored streamers and so on.